Beyond the Stars
The Other Side, Through a Child's Eyes

Beyond the Stars
The Other Side, Through a Child's Eyes

Listen very carefully!

Story and Illustrations
Joan M. Hellquist

Edited by
Nathaniel Lukas

Beyond the Stars
The Other Side, Through a Child's Eyes

Bear Foot Printing

Bear Foot Printing
A Division of Artistic Endeavors
P.O. Box 95
Placitas, NM 87043
www.joanmhellquist.com
beyondthestars1975@gmail.com

Dedication

To Jamie for being a gift,

a blessing and

a catalyst

and

To Bob for your love,

strength and

forgiveness.

As Jamie walked into the meadow, she saw the polar bear cub that her grandpa had mentioned. He was playing in the flowers on the hill across the lush field of grass. The little bear was running up the hill and then somersaulting all the way to the bottom. As he went head-over-heels down to the valley floor, he created an explosion of white blossoms. He'd sit there briefly and then scamper up to the top again. As he headed back up, the wide path where he'd flattened the flowers filled in like it had never been touched. Jamie thought that was odd.

She reached the bottom of his path and waited until he came to a stop right in front of her. His fur looked like it had changed to flowers.

"Hi Bear," Jamie said.

"Uh…hi," said the little bear, somewhat startled, as he had not seen her coming.

"My name is Jamie and I just got here. What's your name?"

The little bear stood up on all fours and shook himself, sending the flowers stuck in his fur flying off onto the ground.

"My name is Nanuayaaq, but you just called me Bear and I kinda like that. Nanuayaaq means little polar bear. That's what I am. I'm just a cub, but you calling me Bear makes me feel BIG. And that feels good," said the young bear.

"Okay, I'll call you Bear," said Jamie.

"You said you just got here?" asked Bear.

"I think so," Jamie replied. "Time seems funny here."

"It is. That is one of many things that are different about this place," said Bear. "How did you find me?"

"Grandpa told me that you were playing over here and he thought we'd like to play together," explained Jamie.

"Oh, I know your grandpa. He's a nice man. He said that you were coming. Did your grandpa meet you at the gate?" asked Bear.

"Yes," said Jamie, "and he told me that he knew I was coming too, but I don't know how. Did someone meet you when you got here?"

"Aana, that means Grandma, met me. Aana knew I was coming too. Everyone here knows a lot. I know more here than I did there. We all do. This is a very special place."

Jamie wondered how all of that could be: that when you arrive here, you all of a sudden know a lot of things that you weren't ever told or taught.

"Bear, I have a lot of questions. Will you please help me?" Jamie asked. She felt somewhat lost in this new place that was very big and beautiful.

"Let's go over and sit under those trees and I'll try to answer your questions," said Bear.

As Bear trotted over to the large trees, Jamie skipped along beside him. He'd never seen anyone skip before. Bear wondered if he could learn to do that too. He thought it looked like fun.

Jamie started questioning Bear nonstop. "Where are we? What is the name of this place? How did I get here? Why am I here? How long will I..."

"Wait!" interrupted Bear. "Please, ask one question at a time."

"Oh, I'm sorry Bear. I'm just so excited. What is this place called?"

"Aana says it has lots of names. And some people are surprised that this place is really here. But it is here and so are we," said Bear, smiling, as the two friends arrived at the trees and sat down.

"Grandpa called it a land of peace, joy and love," said Jamie. "Is that one of its names?"

"It is a land of peace, joy and love because we have all of those things here," Bear answered. "The names I can remember are Heaven, the Spirit World and the Other Side."

"Where are we?" Jamie asked.

"We are way out beyond the stars, but also next to the people, or bears, who love us," he answered.

"I don't understand," Jamie said. "How can we be far away and also close at the same time?"

"That's just the way it is," Bear said with a grin.

"How do you know all of this, Bear?" asked Jamie.

"Aana tells it all to me. She is very isumatu, uh, wise. When we get here, someone tells us these things, like your grandpa and my aana."

"The light is odd here and there aren't any shadows. Is that because we are beyond the stars?" asked Jamie.

"Yes, the light comes from all of those stars up there in the sky. They are our suns. Some are closer than others, and we don't have just one like the earth does."

Jamie paused a few seconds and asked, "Why am I here? Did I do something wrong so that I couldn't stay with Mommy and Daddy?"

"No, Jamie, you didn't do anything wrong. Everyone comes here at different times for different reasons. Sometimes we get really sick or hurt or very old. But no matter what the reason is, Aana says that we come at our time."

"I think I was born too little. I hadn't been in my mommy long enough to be okay in the Earth Place. Is that what it is called there, the Earth Place?"

Bear replied, "Aana calls it being on Earth. I got sick on Earth so that's why it was my time. Then I came here."

"I didn't even get to know Mommy and Daddy. Well, I did get to know Mommy a little, since I was in her tummy. And I heard them talking. Will I ever see Mommy and Daddy?" Jamie asked. She was suddenly aware of how much she wanted to see her parents and be able to talk to them.

"Sure," said Bear, "you can see them anytime you want. Just close your eyes. Go ahead, close them."

"All I can see is black," Jamie said as she held her eyes tightly shut.

"Okay, now that you've closed your eyes, picture what your parents look like," Bear said to Jamie. "Can you see them now?" he asked.

"Yes, yes, I see them!" exclaimed Jamie.

"Now that you can see them, open your eyes," said Bear. Jamie did just that. "Can you still see them?" Bear asked.

"Yes, I can still see them!" said Jamie. "But they aren't there, they're right HERE! Can you see them too, Bear?"

"No, Jamie," Bear replied "You are the only one who can see them. And they usually can't see us, either. But sometimes people or animals on Earth can learn to see us."

"They both look so sad! They're crying! What's wrong?" Jamie exclaimed. She had no idea why her parents were so heartbroken.

"They're sad because you aren't there with them and they miss you," said Bear.

"I don't want them to be sad. Don't they know I'm okay here?"

"No they don't. They don't know how you're feeling or where you are. They only know that you aren't with them anymore," explained Bear.

"Can I talk to them to tell them I'm okay? I don't want them to worry about me," she said.

"Sure you can," said Bear. "Just go ahead and talk to them."

"Will they hear me?" asked Jamie

"If they listen very carefully, they will," answered Bear.

"Mommy, Daddy, it's me, Jamie. I'm here and I'm okay. Grandpa met me at the gate and I have a new friend, Bear. Please don't be sad. I love you." Jamie looked hopeful but inside she felt unsure as to whether or not her parents were going to be able to hear her.

Then Jamie asked Bear, "Do I need to come here to these trees to be able to see and talk to Mommy and Daddy?"

"No," said Bear, "you can see and talk to them anywhere you are here. Now that you know how, you can do it anytime."

"Wow, that's great!" said Jamie. "I'm going to talk to them a lot until they hear me and then they won't be so sad. Was your family on Earth sad when you first got here?"

"My aaka, that means mama, and Malgi, my twin, were very, very sad when I first got here. They both cried a lot, especially Aaka. Malgi tried to comfort her, but she still cried."

"So Malgi didn't get sick like you did?" asked Jamie.

"No, he didn't, just me."

"Are they still very sad?" asked Jamie.

"As soon as Aaka and Malgi learned how to hear me and we talked, they weren't sad anymore. They just miss me now. I talk to them a lot and that helps," he explained.

"That must be wonderful," said Jamie. "I can't wait until my parents hear me and talk to me too. Then maybe they won't be so unhappy."

"Don't worry, Jamie, they will hear you and it will happen sooner than you think."

Jamie was reassured by Bear's story. She sat under the trees thinking about this wonderful new place around her. Bear was really nice and also she felt safe around him, but she wasn't exactly sure why she felt that way.

A puzzling thought came to her and she said out loud, "So you said you are a polar bear..."

"Yes, I'm a polar bear," Bear interrupted.

"Well. don't polar bears live where it's really cold?" asked Jamie.

"Yes, I'm from the northern coast of Alaska, above the Arctic Circle," answered Bear. "That's where the Inupiaq people live. Nanuayaaq is my Inupiaq name."

"But it isn't cold in this place! And when I came over to you, you were rolling down that hill of flowers," said Jamie.

"Yes, I was and it was lots of fun!" said Bear.

Jamie continued to wonder out loud, "I'm a little girl wearing shorts and a tee shirt and I'm comfortable. And you're a polar bear and you have a lot of fur. Are you comfortable too?"

"Yup," replied Bear.

"How can that be?" asked Jamie.

"Here the temperature and everything else is perfect for everyone, no matter where they lived on Earth. That is another reason this is a very special place."

"You're a polar bear and I'm a little girl. I'm not afraid of you and you are being very nice to me and not trying to hurt me...." Jamie continued to ponder, "Is that another special thing?"

"Yup," said Bear. "And here is another. Are you hungry?"

Jamie thought about that for a few seconds and said, "No, I'm not hungry."

"We don't eat here," said Bear. "And because we don't eat, no one hurts anyone else," he explained. "On Earth, polar bears eat seals. Here I can be friends with seals. On Earth your parents would tell you to stay away from polar bears, lions, tigers, snakes and all sorts of animals that are scary there. Here you can be friends with all of us. No one will hurt you."

Bear smiled. "I want you to meet a friend of mine. Her name is Cotton."

"Cotton, please come here," said Bear. "I want you to meet my new friend, Jamie." Bear seemed to just ask his request out into the air, not aiming his call in any direction or using a loud voice. Jamie wondered how this *Cotton* would hear him.

Jamie turned and saw a blur of brown fur hopping through the blue flowers on the hillside by the trees. "What's that over there?" she asked.

"Oh, that's Cotton," said Bear. "She's a rabbit."

"A polar bear and a rabbit are friends here?" asked Jamie with wonder. "This place certainly is different. How did she hear you when you called? You didn't yell."

"If we want someone to come to us here, we just think about them and ask them to come. And they do," explained Bear.

Cotton hopped over to them and said, "Hi, Nanuayaaq."

"Hi Cotton," replied Bear. "I'd like you to meet Jamie. She just got here and I'm telling her about things."

Cotton jumped up onto Bear's back and sat down on his shoulders. Then looking directly at Jamie, she said, "Hi Jamie."

"Hi Cotton," said Jamie, "You look a little funny sitting up there on Bear's shoulders. He looks like he has four ears now."

"I really like sitting up here on Nanuayaaq's, uh, Bear's shoulders. It makes me feel tall!" Cotton explained.

"Cotton seems to have a thing about sitting on the shoulders of her friends. You'd better watch out, Jamie, because she'll be on your shoulders soon," said Bear.

"That would be okay, I wouldn't mind," said Jamie.

"Jamie, I like that you call Nanuayaaq 'Bear.' It is much easier to say," Cotton said smiling. And then she asked, "Instead of your shoulders, Jamie, may I lie down on your lap?"

"Sure," answered Jamie. It only took Cotton one little hop and she was airborne, headed for Jamie's lap.

As Cotton was in midair, Jamie said, "Oh, look at your tail! No wonder your name is Cotton! Your tail looks like a big, fluffy ball of cotton."

"Yes, I'm a cottontail rabbit," she said as she settled onto Jamie's lap. "I'd like to tell you a story. May I?"

"Sure, I love stories," said Jamie.

"My family and I lived near a nice lady's house in a desert area by some mountains," said Cotton. "Jamie, you remind me of that lady. She helped me get to this place," explained Cotton.

"You mean when it was your time?" Jamie asked.

"Yes," replied Cotton, "I remember being up by the road and something hit me. It was a car, I think. I was very dizzy and my insides didn't feel right. I was lying near the side of the road. Then the kind lady walked up to me. I guess she thought it was odd that I didn't hop away from her like I usually did."

"Did you know this lady?" asked Jamie.

"I saw her everyday when she went outside with her dogs. She would see me and smile. I could tell she liked me. That day when I was hurt, she talked quietly to me and reached out and touched my fur. I didn't move. She petted my fur and said something to me. I couldn't understand her words. Then she walked back to her house. I wanted her to come back to where I was so badly, because I knew it was close to my time and I didn't want to be alone."

"Did she come back?" Jamie asked, already very concerned for her new friend.

"Yes, she did. In just a few minutes she came back to me with a towel. She picked me up and put me on the soft towel and carried me into her house. She sat down on a big chair and held me on the towel on her lap, just like you are holding me right now." The young rabbit had tears welling up in her eyes as she remembered feeling safe and comforted by the kind lady.

Cotton continued, "The lady spoke to me quietly and then her littlest dog, I think she called her Mahtha, jumped up on the seat of the chair beside us. The little dog nuzzled me with her nose and was also very gentle with me. I think Mahtha could also tell that it was almost my time."

Then Cotton said in a very soft voice, "A few minutes after that, I found myself here. It was just like going to sleep. The only thing I didn't understand was why the lady had tears running down her cheeks while she held me."

"She knew it was your time and she loved you," Bear said with a shaky voice.

Cotton tucked her chin down toward her chest and said in a voice so quiet that Jamie and Bear could barely hear her, "I loved her too."

Jamie and Bear were unable to hold back their own tears. All three sat quietly for a few minutes under the trees. And although at first they felt sad, their sadness was gradually replaced by stronger feelings of peace, love and friendship.

Then Jamie asked, "Cotton, why do I remind you of that lady?"

"Well, you sort of look like her. You're a little girl, not a grown lady, but I can tell you love animals. That lady loved all of the animals. Well, almost all of them, I guess. She didn't seem to like snakes. I didn't like them either, but the lady was good to all of us, even the snakes."

"That's a really nice story, Cotton," said Jamie, "Thank you for sharing it with me."

"You're welcome, Jamie," Cotton replied, as she hopped off Jamie's lap and sat in the grass.

"I have another question for you, Cotton," Jamie said.

"What is it?" answered Cotton.

"Do you have problems with animals like snakes here?"

"No," replied Cotton, "I don't have a problem with anyone here. In fact, another of my good friends here is Cromwell."

"What kind of animal is Cromwell?" asked Jamie.

"He's a crocodile!" said Cotton with a big grin on her face. "I sit on his back and he takes me for rides all over the swamp. We have so much fun!"

"You have a swamp here?" asked Jamie.

"We have swamps, jungles, mountains, oceans and deserts. We even have ice floes for Nanuayaaq, sorry, uh, Bear, for whenever he wants to feel like he's home in the Arctic," explained Cotton.

"Wow, that is really neat!" said Jamie. "And I guess the swamp would be lots of fun because the animals aren't scary like they are on Earth. I'd like to meet Cromwell."

"You will!" said Cotton, grinning as she thought about her fun with her reptile friend in the swamp.

"Everyone is so nice to each other. Is that just the way it is here?" asked Jamie.

"You remember that your grandpa calls this a place of peace, joy and love, right?" asked Bear.

"Yes," replied Jamie.

"Well, nobody fights here. Nobody argues here, either. Nobody ever gets sick and nobody gets hurt. We all love each other. Aana says that if we love, we feel joy, and if we feel joy and love each other, it is peaceful place," Bear explained.

"I think your aana and Jamie's grandpa have been talking to each other," said Cotton.

"Yeah, I think they have," said Jamie. "This place is really great! If only Mommy and Daddy were here with me."

"They will be someday," said Bear. "Usually we get to greet them at the gate when it is their time, just like your grandpa greeted you."

The three friends were quiet for a while, feeling grateful for being together in such a special place. Then Bear said, "Why don't we go back to the white flowers? I really like them a lot. There weren't any hills of flowers where I lived in Alaska."

All three got up and headed over toward the base of the hill of white flowers. As Bear walked, Jamie skipped beside him. Cotton, as usual, rode on Bear's shoulders.

While they were on their way to the flowers, Jamie said, "Bear, why did you say the word *usually* when you told me about greeting my parents at the gate?"

"Well," said Bear, "some of us arrive before we have finished doing all of our work on Earth. In that case, Aana says that our soul can go back to Earth to finish the work."

"What is a soul?" asked Jamie.

"Our soul is who we really are inside," said Bear. "It is who we are in our heart. A soul is something that can't be seen. It doesn't have anything to do with whether our fur is white, brown or black or whether we speak English or Bear. Does that make sense?"

"I think I get it, sort of," said Jamie. "Grandpa said he really wanted me to meet my Uncle Oscar, but that I had to wait because he was down on Earth again. So, that means my uncle's SOUL is on Earth again, right?"

"Yup," said Bear, "and he probably has a different name."

"Grandpa said Uncle Oscar was a loyal and caring man and a brave American soldier. So that would mean that he is still loyal, caring and brave, but he may not live in America or be a soldier. Is that right?" Jamie asked.

"Exactly right," said Bear.

"Does everybody have to go back to Earth?" asked Jamie.

"No, not everyone goes back, only those who want to," Bear replied.

The three reached the bottom of the hill of flowers and sat down side by side.

"Wow," said Jamie. "I still have so many questions about this place. I hope you two don't mind me asking you so many."

Cotton said, "We don't mind, Jamie. But we probably don't know the answers to all of your questions, so some you'll need to ask your grandpa."

"Well, here's another one that maybe you can answer," said Jamie. "I know that on Earth lots of people have pets like dogs, cats, birds, horses and fish. Mommy and Daddy have a dog. His name is Blitz. When it is Blitz's time, will he come here too?"

"Oh yes! Pets come here too and they are greeted by their families just like we are. You will probably greet Blitz. I have heard that when it is a pet's time to come here that their family on Earth is very sad," said Bear.

"Well, a pet is a family member so it must be very sad. When Blitz comes here, will he be able to hear Mommy and Daddy talk to him too?" asked Jamie.

"Yes, Blitz will be able to hear them," said Cotton.

"Everyone here can learn to talk to family members on Earth."

Jamie sat thinking about all of the people and pets and wild animals and said, "This place must be REALLY BIG for everyone to be able to fit here! But I don't see anybody else but us."

"Yes, Jamie," said Bear. "This is a VERY BIG place! Everyone can be in their own area with as many or as few people or animals as they want around them."

For a few minutes, Jamie sat there daydreaming about the size of this special place.

Then her eyes got really big and she said, "I think I just heard my mommy!"

"What did she say?" asked Cotton.

"She said that she hoped I wasn't suffering and that I was okay...that she misses me and loves me. That is another word I don't know. What does suffering mean?"

"I think it means hurting a lot," answered Cotton, "I remember the kind lady using that word when she talked to me."

"Why would Mommy and the kind lady think we were hurting a lot?" asked Jamie.

"Because they don't know where we are or that we're here in this very special place," replied Bear.

Jamie closed her eyes and said, "I'm not hurting at all here, Mommy, please know that." She concentrated really hard, "Mommy and Daddy," she said, "I love you, too."

"Can you tell if they heard you?" Bear asked.

"I can't tell if they heard me or not," Jamie said to her new friends. She hoped that she and her parents would be able to talk very soon.

The white flowers felt cool against the palms of Jamie's hands and they tickled her ankles. Bear and Cotton were there by her side watching over her. They remembered how it was to be new in this place and wanted to help her as much as they could.

Then Jamie said, "I have another question. If my time was just after I was born, why am I a little girl here in this place and not a baby?"

"I'll answer that one," said Cotton. "Everyone here takes care of themselves. If you were a baby you wouldn't be able to do that. If you were very old, you might not be able to do that either. So here we are an age that we can take care of ourselves. And if you had a disability of any kind on Earth, when you get here, it's gone. That way you can take care of yourself."

Jamie thought that made a lot of sense.

"I still have another question for you, Bear," Jamie said. "When I walked over here earlier, you were rolling down this hill. It looked like the flowers were bent over where you rolled. But when you ran up the hill, they looked like they stood up again. Did they?"

"They did! I'll show you," said Bear.

He walked up into the flowers on the side of the hill. Jamie wasn't sure what was about to happen. "Look at this, Jamie!" said Bear. He lay down on his back and then with his four huge paws up in the air he rolled from side to side to flatten the flowers.

Then Bear jumped to his feet and exclaimed, "There! They're all squished!" He grinned, very proud of himself, and said, "Now watch."

One by one, each of the little white flowers popped upright until they all looked as if they had never been touched!

"That is so cool!" said Jamie. "You must be a magician."

"It's not me, it's this place," Bear said with a wise and gentle smile.

"Here's an even better trick," he said. Bear grabbed a paw-full of white flowers. With a quick movement, he pulled the stems of the flowers and they broke off right at the ground.

Just as Jamie was about to say, "Oh no!" new flowers with stems immediately took the place of the picked ones.

"Wow!" said Jamie, "It looks like another magic trick. These little flowers are so pretty! I love them. I can see in the distance some more hills of flowers. Some of them have blue flowers and others have pink.

"They are all the same kind of flowers, just different colors," explained Bear.

"Let's play in the flowers!" said Cotton.

"Okay!" Jamie replied, and all three dived into the white carpet of blossoms.

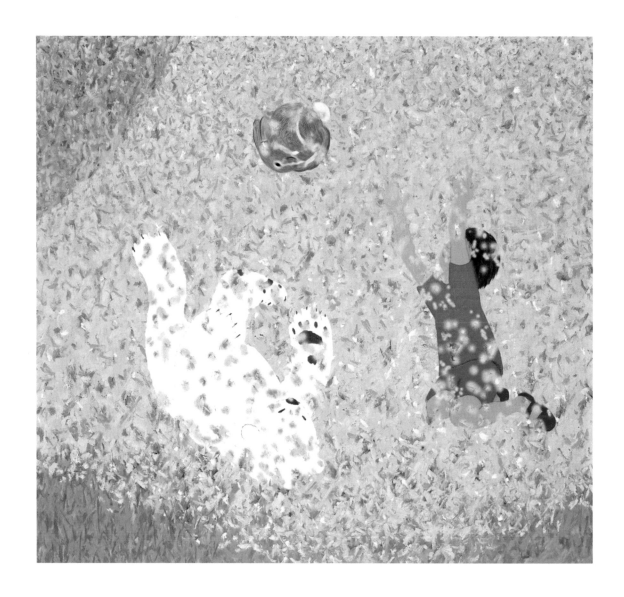

Bear was on his back, picking flowers and throwing them up into the air. As soon as he did so, new flowers would appear. Jamie was throwing flowers in the air too, watching them fall like snow all over. Meanwhile Cotton was hopping around and doing flips. The three of them giggled so much that they were almost crying with joy.

After several minutes of playing, they plopped back into the sea of white flowers. Jamie and Bear were on their backs holding hand and paw with Cotton lying right between them.

"Wow, that was so much fun!" said Jamie. "Thank you both for being my friends."

"You're welcome, Jamie," said Bear.

"I'm happy to have a new friend," Cotton added.

"Me too," said Bear.

They all lay there for several minutes. Then Jamie said to Bear, "You told me that these white flowers are the same kind of flowers as the pink and blue ones on the other hills, but you haven't told me their name."

Bear smiled and said, "They're called forget-me-nots."

"Forget-me-nots," Jamie said their name so quietly that Bear and Cotton couldn't hear. "That's perfect." She smiled and felt very happy and safe.

Knowing the name of the flowers made Jamie REALLY want to talk to her parents and have them hear her.

"I'm going to talk to Mommy and Daddy again," Jamie announced.

"That's good, Jamie," said Bear, "the more often you do it, the faster they'll learn how to hear you."

Jamie closed her eyes and pictured her mommy and daddy. Then she opened her eyes and said, "Don't be sad, Mommy and Daddy. I'm happy here with Bear, Cotton and Grandpa. I'm safe and I don't hurt at all here. You can talk to me anytime and if you listen very, very carefully you can hear me talking to you too. I miss you, I love you and I will never forget you. Please don't ever forget me, either."

Jamie waited and waited for what seemed to be forever. She didn't hear anything and said very quietly, "I guess it will be a very long time before Mommy and Daddy hear me talk to them."

Jamie's friends saw how sad she was and went to her side. Bear put his huge paw gently on Jamie's back and Cotton held onto Jamie's arm with her soft front paws.

Bear said, "We're sorry that you are so sad and disappointed right now. This can take some time. What can we do to help you?"

"I don't know," replied Jamie, in a small voice.

Cotton remembered how she had felt before her family on Earth heard her. She said to Jamie, "I cried sometimes because I wanted my family to hear me so badly. I almost lost hope. But then all of a sudden they did hear me and we've been talking to each other ever since! My mama and papa are here now, but I still talk with my cousins who are on Earth. I even talk with the kind lady sometimes. Your parents will hear you soon, Jamie. I know they will!"

Jamie's eyes were filling with tears as she let her chin rest on her chest. She wanted to talk to her parents so much.

And then, suddenly, Jamie heard, "We hear you, Jamie! It's Mommy and Daddy! We love you and miss you too and of course we'll never forget you!"

Jamie immediately jumped up on her feet and ran up the hill exclaiming with joy, "Mommy and Daddy, you hear me!" She got up on her toes and reached up with both of her arms. Her sad look had turned into a big smile.

As she stood there, not far from her friends, Jamie seemed to be hugging the air. However, Bear and Cotton could tell she was hugging her parents. And the look on Jamie's face told them that she was feeling her parents hugging her back.

Bear and Cotton were very happy for Jamie and left her alone during this special time.

After a few minutes Jamie said, "Wow! That felt sooo good! They told me they will talk to me often and send lots of hugs. It feels like now I can talk to them anytime and they can do the same!"

"You can," said Bear. "And you felt them hug you too, didn't you?"

"Yes, and it was great!" exclaimed Jamie.

The three friends wanted to celebrate what Jamie had just experienced for the first time. They walked down the hill of white flowers into the grassy meadow.

Although Bear suggested that maybe a dance would be a good way to share their joy, Jamie asked if they could have their own group hug instead. So Bear and Jamie stepped toward each other and Cotton jumped up into their arms. They all thought it was wonderful to feel as physically close to each other as they felt in their hearts.

Since that time, Bear and Cotton have introduced Jamie to Cromwell and several other friends and family members. The three best friends continue their special relationship in the beautiful land of peace, joy and love.

Jamie, Bear and Cotton never get tired of playing in the flowers with the perfect name. And when Blitz arrived, Jamie met him at the gate and immediately introduced him to her two best buddies. Now they ALL play together in the little white flowers.

Jamie talks with her parents and other family members often. They have all learned how this form of communication works and now they can see each other, too. Most importantly Jamie's parents know that she is safe and happy playing with her friends and family in that special place beyond the stars.

Jamie's parents will certainly never forget her. They love her very much and they will always miss her, but the extreme sadness they once felt has lessened a great deal. And for that, they are very grateful.

Maybe Bear was correct after all, that beyond the stars and next to those who love us, are the same place? Could that be true?

"You'll be with me like a handprint on my heart."
Stephen Schwartz

Acknowledgements

For Good

From the Broadway Musical WICKED

Music and Lyrics by Stephen Schwartz

Copyright © 2003 Stephen Schwartz

All Rights Reserved   Used by Permission of Grey Dog Music (ASCAP)

Reprinted by Permission of Hal Leonard Corporation

To Daniel J. Cox who introduced me to Bear, Bear's aaka and Malgi in powerful sequential photos in his book, *BEAR: A Celebration of Power and Beauty*, A Sierra Club Book, San Francisco, 2000. They brought tears to my eyes when I first saw them in your book while in Churchill, MB in 2005 and they still do.

To Flora M. Rexford for her help with the words from her Inupiaq language and for sharing with me her beautiful artwork and way of life on Barter Island in Alaska.

Much love and thanks to Bob, Jamie, Bear, Bear's aaka and Cotton. And to Jamie's older and younger siblings who didn't make it as far along as she did.

Love and special thanks to Sue who so unexpectedly pointed out to me that I had not properly grieved the loss of my daughter.   You also let me know that I hadn't dealt with a lot of other losses in this lifetime and many past lifetimes. This book would not exist without your love, understanding and guidance.

Thanks to all whose time has already come. To Mom and Dad and all other family members that I knew and loved and to those I have never met. And thanks to Ann, Becky, Cindy, David, Eddie, Gail, Kathy, Olivia, Ouida, Patti, Peter and Polly...all very special friends who also live in that special place beyond the stars.

To Barre, much love and thanks for helping me when I most needed it, for your understanding and for being the best brother ever.

Marion, I know you would have enjoyed this if things hadn't progressed so quickly for you. Thank you for being such a wonderful wife for Barre, mother for Eric and Paul and sister-in-law for me.

To Paula, much love and thanks for being there for me when this loss occurred. How I wish you could be here for me now. You know how I feel about you and I'll see you again, beyond the stars.

Thanks to all of you, friends and family, who have read this during its early and more recent drafts. And thanks to all of you who have been support and helped me get this book into its final form. To Avi and Steve, Anne and Doris, Anne and Sarah, Betsy, Bev and Joyce, Beverly, Brian and Kathy, Bob and Hope, Carol, Cecilia, Cindy, Darwin and Ouida, Deb, Dr. H, Eric and Jess, George and Marcia, Heather and Rick, Irene, Jeff and Linda, Jennifer, Joanne, Kristina, Lukas, Marie, Maurine, Marion K, Marla, Maryl, Maranda, Mauryne, Meg, Merrily, Michelle and Paul, Morgan, Pat and Toni, Patti, Sherry, Siegfried, Simyra and Victor.

About the Author

Joan M. Hellquist has always been a storyteller. This is her first book and although it is a work of fiction, the characters and even the flowers are real because Joan has experienced them in reality or during meditation.

Joan grew up in Summit, New Jersey. She has lived in eight states, but feels very much at home in Placitas, New Mexico where she has been since 1988. Joan worked in healthcare for almost twenty years. Since 2001, she has pursued her artwork, painting pastel landscapes and wildlife images on American Indian-made hand drums. Joan is also a Service Dog trainer. She and her dog, Piki, train Service Dogs to work with children with disabilities. This combines her love of both children and animals.

Made in the USA
Columbia, SC
28 June 2017